American Biographies

ABRAHAM LINCOLN

Elizabeth Raum

Chicago, Illinois

www.capstonepub.com
Visit our website to find out more information about Heinemann-Raintree books.

To order:

☎ Phone 800-747-4992

▣ Visit www.capstonepub.com to browse our catalog and order online.

Edited by Abby Colich, Megan Cotugno, and Laura Hensley
Designed by Philippa Jenkins
Original illustrations © Capstone Global Library Limited 2011
Illustrated by Oxford Designers and Illustrators
Picture research by Tracy Cummins
Originated by Capstone Global Library Limited
Printed and bound in China by Leo Paper Group

15 14 13 12
10 9 8 7 6 5 4 3 2 1

Library of Congress Cataloging-in-Publication Data
Raum, Elizabeth.
  Abraham Lincoln / Elizabeth Raum.
    p. cm.—(American biographies)
  Includes bibliographical references and index.
  ISBN 978-1-4329-6453-5 (hb)—ISBN 978-1-4329-6464-1 (pb) 1. Lincoln, Abraham, 1809-1865—Juvenile literature. 2. Presidents—United States—Biography—Juvenile literature. I. Title.
  E457.905.R38 2013
  973.7092—dc23   2011037577
  [B]

Acknowledgments
The author and publishers are grateful to the following for permission to reproduce copyright material: Corbis: pp. 8 (© Morton Beebe), 20 (© Bettmann), 23 (© Bettmann), 27 (© CORBIS); Getty Images: pp. 11 (George Eastman House), 13 (Kean Collection), 36 (Stock Montage), 37 (MPI); Library of Congress Prints & Photographs Division: pp. 4, 9, 10, 14, 19, 21, 24, 25, 26, 29, 30, 31, 32, 33, 35, 38, 39, 40; North Wind Picture Archives: p. 18 (© North Wind); Picture History: p. 17; Shutterstock: pp. 5 (© schankz), 15 (© Chas), 41 (© Norbert Rehm); The Granger Collections, NYC: p. 34.

Cover image of Abraham Lincoln portrait reproduced with permission from the Library of Congress Prints and Photographs Division.

Every effort has been made to contact copyright holders of material reproduced in this book. Any omissions will be rectified in subsequent printings if notice is given to the publisher.

Contents

Some words are shown in bold, **like this**.
These words are explained in the glossary.

Lincoln Today

Abraham Lincoln was not a handsome man. Many people considered him ugly. U.S. poet Walt Whitman, who often saw President Lincoln in Washington, D.C., said that Lincoln's face was "so awful ugly it becomes beautiful." Today, most Americans carry his picture around in their pockets—on their money.

Lincoln was president when this photo was taken in 1864.

It was not only Lincoln's face that was unusual. He was 6 feet, 4 inches (about 2 meters) tall and weighed 200 pounds (90 kilograms). The average man at the time was 5 feet, 7 inches (1.7 meters) tall, so Lincoln towered over other men. Years of hard work had made him strong, too. Even his hands were large and muscular. Two hundred years later, Lincoln still towers over many others as an important figure in United States history.

Lincoln's fame

Many experts consider Abraham Lincoln one of the most important presidents of the United States. He is admired throughout the world. More than 14,000 books have been written about Lincoln since his death in 1865. Dozens of movies tell the story of his life and times. Towns and cities have been named after him. Illinois calls itself the "Land of Lincoln," and dozens of companies use Lincoln's name as a way of claiming that they are as honest as "Honest Abe."

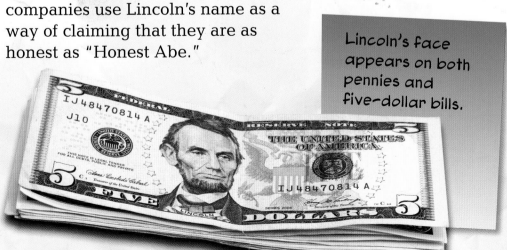

Lincoln's face appears on both pennies and five-dollar bills.

Country Boyhood

For many people, Abraham Lincoln's life is proof that in the United States anything is possible. Born in a log cabin on the Kentucky frontier, he grew up to become the most powerful man in the nation. His parents, Thomas and Nancy, could not read and write. Abraham himself had less than a year of schooling.

ILLINOIS

New Salem Decatur

Springfield

INDIANA

Spencer County

Hodgenville

KENTUCKY

This map shows Lincoln's homes from his birth until his election as president.

Abraham Lincoln was born on Sinking Spring Farm, near the present-day town of Hodgenville, Kentucky, (see the map) on February 12, 1809. He lived in a one-room log cabin with a dirt floor and stone fireplace. When Abraham was two, Thomas and Nancy Lincoln moved their family 6 miles (9.6 kilometers) north to Knob Creek Valley. Abraham helped his father grow corn and beans. His sister, Sarah, was two years older. His brother, Thomas, who was three years younger, died a few days after being born.

Schooling

At age six, Abraham hiked 4 miles (6.4 kilometers) to attend a one-room school. Like many frontier schools, it opened for only a few weeks at a time whenever the settlers could hire a teacher. Even so, Abraham learned to read, write, and count to 10.

Did you know?

The school Abraham attended was called a "blab school." Students learned by reading out loud and repeating the lessons over and over. Lincoln read aloud as an adult, too. He said, "When I read aloud two senses catch the idea: first, I see what I read; second, I hear it, and therefore I can remember it better."

The Lincolns lived in this tiny cabin in Little Pigeon Creek, Indiana.

Moving to Indiana

In 1816, when Abraham was seven, the Lincolns moved to Indiana (see the map on page 6). Thomas Lincoln was looking for good farmland. He also disliked **slavery**. Slavery was legal in Kentucky, but not in Indiana. Abraham's father taught him to use an ax. Then he put Abraham to work chopping wood, clearing the land, and splitting logs to make fences. Abraham grew strong and powerful, but he never enjoyed physical labor. Because Abraham seemed happiest when reading and thinking, some people said that he was lazy.

Abraham's mothers

In 1818 Abraham's mother, Nancy, died. Abraham's sister, Sarah, who was 11 at the time, tried to manage the household and help with the farm as her mother had done. But it was too much. The children needed a mother, and Thomas needed a wife. So Thomas married Sarah Bush Johnston, a **widow** with three children. They moved into the tiny cabin. Thomas put in a new floor, fixed the roof, and added some beds. Sarah Bush Johnson brought order to the household and became a loving mother to Abraham. She considered him well behaved. He rose early, went to bed early, and tried to do whatever his mother asked.

Abraham's stepmother said, "He [Abraham] read all the books he could lay his hands on."

Did you know?

When Abraham was about eight years old, he borrowed his father's gun and shot a wild turkey. When he saw the beautiful bird lying dead, he was overcome with sadness. He never shot another one.

By the time he was 16, Abraham earned 25 cents a day splitting logs.

A natural leader

When Abraham was 10 years old, he attended school for another month or two. However, he mostly taught himself. When he wrestled, raced, and played games with other boys, he was usually the leader. People liked him. Abraham knew how to make people laugh.

When Abraham was 13 or 14, Thomas Lincoln sent him to work harvesting corn or splitting fence rails for other farmers. Abraham gave his earnings to his father. When Abraham was 17, he built a flat-bottomed boat to use on the Ohio River. When two men asked if he could row them out to their ship, he quickly agreed. The men paid him a dollar. It was one of his proudest days.

Traveling

When Abraham was 17, a local storeowner hired him to transport goods by river to New Orleans to sell. Abraham traveled with Allen Gentry, the storeowner's son. They took supplies 1,222 miles (1,967 kilometers) along the Ohio and Mississippi rivers on a **flatboat**. New Orleans was the first city Abraham had ever seen. He spent about three days there before taking a steamboat home.

In 1830 Thomas Lincoln moved his family to Illinois, 225 miles (362 kilometers) northwest. At 21 years of age, Abraham was old enough to leave home, but he stayed to help the family get settled on a farm near Decatur (see the map on page 6).

Lincoln traveled to New Orleans on a flatboat loaded with supplies.

Store Clerk and Soldier

The next year, 1831, Abraham Lincoln set out on his own for New Salem, Illinois, a town of about 100 people (see the map on page 6). Lincoln made friends easily, and he was soon offered another chance to go to New Orleans. This time he made a trading trip for New Salem storeowner Denton Offutt. When he returned, Lincoln became a clerk at Offutt's store. He shared a room at the back with another clerk. When the store was empty, Lincoln read.

One day Lincoln wrestled the local strong man. The match ended with Lincoln winning, which earned him the respect of his neighbors. Lincoln also joined the town's debating club. That is where he became friends with a schoolteacher who helped Lincoln improve his speaking and writing skills. In 1832 Lincoln's neighbors encouraged him to run for the Illinois state **legislature**. Lincoln was 23 years old when he began **campaigning**. He promised to work hard if elected.

Soldier

Lincoln's campaign was interrupted by news that a group of Sauk and Fox warriors had crossed the Mississippi River and entered Illinois. These American Indian peoples wanted to reclaim their land. This was the beginning of the Black Hawk War, named for Black Hawk, a Sauk leader. New Salem organized a **militia** to protect itself. The militia elected Lincoln captain. Although the New Salem militia did not fight any battles during the Black Hawk War, Lincoln was proud of his military service.

Lincoln enjoyed visiting with customers at Offutt's store.

NEW SAL
HOME OF ABRAHAM LINCOLN
PLATTED, COPYRIGHTED AND PUBLISHED
DRAWN BY ARTHUR L. BRO
Adopted as Authentic by Old Salem Chautauqua
COPYRIGHT APPLIED FOR. ALL RIGHTS RE
LITHOGRAPHED BY J. W. FRANKS & SONS, PEOR

Politician

Lincoln returned home from the Black Hawk War in July, just two weeks before the election. He gave a few campaign speeches. Although he won 277 of 300 votes in New Salem, he lost the county election because he was not well-known in the other towns in the voting district.

Meanwhile, Offutt's store closed in the spring of 1832. Lincoln returned to splitting rails and working for local farmers. When he was offered part ownership of another store, he accepted the offer. However, the store did so poorly that Lincoln sold his share to his partner, William Berry. When Berry died in 1835, Lincoln was left with **debts** of the partnership.

14

Postmaster and legislator

Lincoln found work as New Salem's **postmaster**. The job suited Lincoln well. Several newspapers arrived in the mail, and Lincoln read them all. He also worked as a **surveyor**, measuring land throughout the county. These jobs allowed Lincoln to meet people throughout the region. When he ran for the state legislature in 1834, Lincoln won easily. He became a leader in his political party, the **Whigs**. Lincoln served in the Illinois legislature for seven years.

Did you know?

Lincoln earned the nickname "Honest Abe" in New Salem. He sold his horse and belongings to raise money to pay his debts. It took him years, but he eventually paid back every cent. The debt was more than $24,000 in today's dollars.

Every year about 400,000 people visit this **replica** of Lincoln's store, located at Lincoln's New Salem State Historic Site in Illinois.

Settling in Springfield

The small town of New Salem, Illinois, was dying. The post office closed. So did stores. Many people packed up and moved to other towns.

Lincoln decided to become a lawyer. He read law books and studied independently. He received a license to practice law in 1836. In the spring of 1837, he packed his bags and moved to the growing city of Springfield, Illinois, 20 miles (32 kilometers) away (see the map on page 6).

Springfield

Lincoln's first stop was at Joshua Speed's general store in Springfield. The young clerk, Joshua Speed (see the box), had heard of Lincoln's work in the state **legislature**. He invited Lincoln to become his roommate.

Lincoln's luck continued when John Todd Stuart, one of Springfield's most successful lawyers, invited Lincoln to join his law firm. Lincoln enjoyed being a lawyer. He tried cases in Springfield. He also traveled more than 500 miles (800 kilometers) on horseback along dirt roads to try cases in **circuit courts**. Lincoln stayed in crowded hotels, sharing a bed or floor space with two or three other lawyers. During this time, Lincoln made many friends and earned a reputation as a great storyteller.

Joshua Fry Speed

(1814–1882)

Joshua Speed was born in Kentucky five years after Lincoln. Speed came from a wealthy family and attended excellent schools. He spent several years in Springfield, but in 1842 he married and moved back to Lexington, Kentucky. Speed became a successful businessman and railroad president. Even though he and Lincoln disagreed about **slavery**, they remained good friends over the years.

Joshua Fry Speed remained a loyal friend throughout Lincoln's life.

Abraham Lincoln married Mary Todd on November 4, 1842. This is a copy of their marriage certificate.

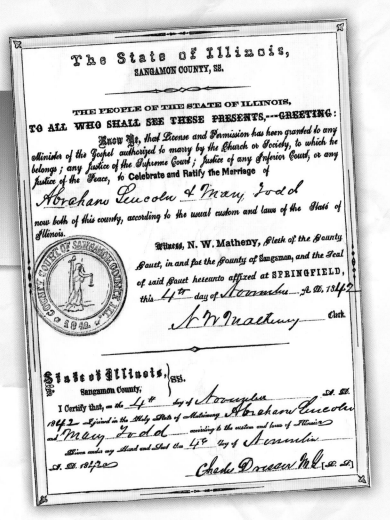

Becoming a family man

Lincoln's sense of humor and intelligence attracted female friends, too. In 1839 he met Mary Todd. Mary was born in Lexington, Kentucky, in 1818. Her father, a wealthy businessman, gave Mary an excellent education. He encouraged her to participate in political discussions. Mary was bright and attractive. Many men wanted to marry her. She chose Abraham Lincoln.

In 1843 Abraham and Mary's first son, Robert Todd Lincoln, was born. They called him Bob. Abraham began calling Mary "Mother," and she called him "Mr. Lincoln." The next year, they moved into their own home. Later they added a second story and extra rooms (see the photo on page 24). In 1846 a second son, Edward Baker Lincoln (called Eddie), was born.

Congressman Lincoln

In 1843 Lincoln ran for the United States Congress. He lost that election, but in 1846, when he ran again, he won. During his two years as a congressman in Washington, D.C., Lincoln borrowed so many books from the Library of Congress that other politicians called him a "bookworm." He listened to hundreds of speeches, too, and gave several of his own. On a speaking tour in Massachusetts, audiences cheered Lincoln's brilliant speeches.

Did you know?

Abraham Lincoln is the only president to receive a **patent** for an invention. In 1849 he invented a new way for steamships to cross sandbars or sail through shallow waters without getting stuck or losing their cargo. This invention was never manufactured.

This 1846 photo is the first ever taken of Abraham Lincoln.

Stirring a Nation

In 1849 Lincoln returned to his law office in Springfield, Illinois. He worked hard, arguing many cases both in Springfield and before **circuit courts**. Lincoln enjoyed family life. However, in February 1850, three-year-old Eddie died after a long illness. Both Abraham and Mary were deeply saddened. Their spirits lifted in December, when William Wallace, called Willie, was born. Three years later a fourth son, Thomas Lincoln, was born. As a baby, Thomas looked like a tadpole, so the family called him "Tad."

Lincoln became a respected lawyer.

Stephen A. Douglas pushed Lincoln back into politics.

Stephen A. Douglas

(1813–1861)

Stephen Arnold Douglas was born in Vermont. At age 20, he moved to Illinois and became a lawyer. Like Lincoln, Douglas had dated Mary Todd and served in the Illinois **legislature** and in the United States Congress. Douglas became a U.S. senator in 1847. In 1860 he ran against Lincoln for president of the United States. Today, Douglas is known for debating Lincoln in 1858 (see page 23). Although Douglas lost the presidency, he supported President Lincoln when the Civil War broke out in 1861. Douglas died a few months later.

Return to politics

In 1854 Illinois senator Stephen A. Douglas (see the box) proposed the Kansas-Nebraska Act to the United States Congress. This act created two new territories—Kansas and Nebraska. It also allowed the settlers of those territories to decide if they would be for or against **slavery**. Lincoln did not like slavery. This act, which threatened to extend slavery, angered Lincoln and brought him back into politics. Like many who were against slavery, Lincoln intended to do everything he could to prevent slavery from spreading.

A new party

Lincoln lost his bid for the United States Senate in 1855. Disappointed, he returned to his law practice. A year later, he helped form the **Republican** Party in Illinois. At first the Republicans had one issue: ending slavery. Eventually they added others, including expanding railroads, improving harbors, and opening the West to settlers. To try to maintain peace, the Republicans agreed to allow slavery to continue in the South, but felt it should not expand beyond that region.

Senate race

In 1858 Lincoln ran for the Senate as a Republican against the **Democrat**, Stephen A. Douglas (see page 21). Lincoln's first speech as candidate became famous. He said, "A house divided against itself cannot stand. I believe this government cannot **endure** permanently half slave and half free." Lincoln feared that disagreements over slavery would tear the nation apart.

The Lincoln-Douglas debates

Lincoln debated Douglas seven times. Each debate lasted more than three hours. Douglas felt slavery was wrong, but he believed that each state should decide for itself. Lincoln disagreed. He referred to the idea in the Declaration of Independence that all men are created equal, saying: "let it be as nearly reached as it can."

Thousands came to the Lincoln-Douglas debates.

Did you know?

Lincoln and Douglas were opposites in looks as well as opinions. Douglas, called the "Little Giant," stood 5 feet, 4 inches (1.6 meters) tall. He had a large head, bushy hair, and a deep voice. Douglas wore fancy, well-fitted clothes. Lincoln, on the other hand, was tall and thin with a high, shrill voice. His jacket and pants were baggy and too short.

Lincoln stands behind a fence at the family's home with sons Willie and Tad in 1860.

Bigger dreams

In 1858 the people of Illinois elected the state legislature, but it was the legislature that then elected U.S. senators. Many thought Lincoln won the debates against Douglas, but the Democrats won the legislature, so they chose Stephen Douglas as senator.

The day after the election, people began suggesting that Lincoln run for president of the United States. He liked the idea. In February 1860, he gave an important speech in New York City. The audience cheered! Lincoln gave several more speeches in the East. By the time he returned home, his supporters were convinced that he could become president.

Fact VS. Fiction

In 1860, 11-year-old Grace Bedell of Westfield, New York, studied a photo of Abraham Lincoln. She thought he would look better with a beard. She wrote a letter telling him so. After the election, Lincoln met Grace. He touched his beard and said, "You see, I let these whiskers grow for you, Grace." It's a fact! From that time on, Lincoln wore a beard.

Running for president

During the presidential election, Lincoln ran against Douglas, who was supported by Democrats in the North, and John C. Breckinridge, who was supported by Democrats in the South. This split among Democrats helped the Republicans win. Lincoln won every northern state except New Jersey (where he tied with Douglas) to become the next president of the United States.

Posters such as this one helped Lincoln get elected president.

Inauguration of Abraham Lincoln – March 4, 1861.

Leaving Springfield

As the Lincoln family boarded a train bound for Washington, D.C., Lincoln told well-wishers in Springfield, "I now leave... with a task before me greater than that which rested upon [George] Washington." When George Washington became president in 1789, the nation had been united. But when Lincoln became president, it was not. Lincoln's goal was to bring the nation back together.

A nation divided

For decades, conflict had grown between the Northern and Southern states over slavery and the rights of the states to make their own decisions about slavery and other issues. The Republicans opposed slavery. When Lincoln, a Republican, won the election, many Southern states decided it was time to leave the **Union**.

By the time Lincoln took office, seven states had **seceded** (left the Union). South Carolina went first, followed by Mississippi, Florida, Alabama, Georgia, Louisiana, and Texas. They set up their own government, called the **Confederate States of America**. Lincoln wanted to save the nation.

When Lincoln became president, his son Robert was 19, Willie was 10, and Tad was 8.

Fact VS. Fiction

The presidential train took 12 days to travel 1,904 miles (3,064 kilometers) from Springfield, Illinois, to Washington, D.C. The train stopped at major cities along the way. When the train reached Philadelphia, Pennsylvania, railroad detective Allan Pinkerton warned Lincoln of a plot to kill him as the train traveled through Baltimore, Maryland. Pinkerton convinced Lincoln to take a smaller train to Washington. Only Pinkerton and one bodyguard went with him. Lincoln arrived safely in Washington, D.C., at 6:00 a.m., 10 hours ahead of schedule. That's a fact!

Freeing the Slaves, Saving a Nation

Confederate forces fired on Fort Sumter, South Carolina, on April 12, 1861. Lincoln had been in office only 40 days. The fort passed from **Union** to Confederate control on April 13. The Civil War had begun.

People panicked. In Washington, D.C., many businesses closed. Confederate flags were flying across the Potomac River in Virginia. Who would defend the capital? Troops from northern states began marching to Washington.

By July 1861, 11 states had left the Union to form the **Confederate States of America.**

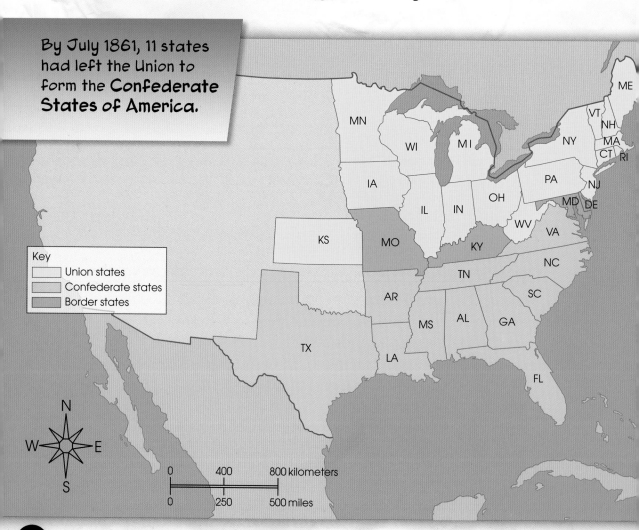

Key
Union states
Confederate states
Border states

N
W — E
S

| 0 | 400 | 800 kilometers |
| 0 | 250 | 500 miles |

Lincoln visited Union troops on the battlefield at Antietam, Maryland.

The battles begin

Lincoln was shocked to find the army and navy unprepared for war. Many soldiers were volunteers who served for only three months. Lincoln appointed General Irwin McDowell to lead the Union troops. The first major battle took place in July 1861, along the Bull Run River in Manassas, Virginia. The fighting lasted 10 hours and left almost 900 men dead. It was a victory for the **Confederacy**.

Lincoln took an active role as commander in chief. He read military books, studied reports from the field, and met with military leaders. After the defeat at Bull Run, Lincoln appointed George B. McClellan as the general in chief of the Union Army. But McClellan disappointed Lincoln. Confederate forces won many battles. They even crossed the Potomac River into Maryland.

Fact VS. Fiction

Congressmen and citizens, supplied with picnic baskets and wine, followed the Union Army to Manassas to watch the battle. This sounds strange, but it is true.

This 1861 painting shows the Lincolns at the White House (from left: Mary Lincoln, Willie, Bob, Tad, and President Lincoln).

Family life

Once the Lincolns settled into the White House, Mary redecorated the **shabby** rooms on the second floor. Bob returned to his studies at Harvard College. Willie and Tad, who loved adventure, played on the White House roof. They painted logs to look like cannons and shot at imaginary Confederate soldiers. People sent them gifts, including a small horse and two goats, Nanko and Nannie.

In the winter of 1862, Willie became ill. He improved a bit, but then he grew worse. On February 20, 1862, 11-year-old Willie died. Mary sobbed endlessly. Tad felt lost without his brother. Abraham comforted them both.

The Emancipation Proclamation

In September 1862 Union troops claimed victory at the Battle of Antietam in Maryland. More than 23,000 soldiers were killed, wounded, or missing after the long, bloody battle. Lincoln warned the Confederate states that if they did not rejoin the Union by January 1, 1863, he would free their slaves.

When they refused, Lincoln issued the **Emancipation** Proclamation. It declared freedom for all slaves in the Confederate states. Lincoln's decision angered white people throughout the Confederacy. The Emancipation Proclamation eventually led to the adoption of the 13th Amendment to the Constitution, which ended **slavery** in the United States.

Abraham Lincoln discussed the Emancipation Proclamation with his closest advisers.

The turning point

For hours every day, Lincoln followed the news from the battlefields. More often than not, the news was bad. However, in June 1863 the Union Army defeated Confederate forces in Gettysburg, Pennsylvania.

Lincoln appointed General Ulysses S. Grant (see box) commander of the Union Army. Grant created a battle plan and coordinated the troops. From that point on, Union victories increased. Grant hammered Confederate troops until they had no choice but to surrender.

Lincoln's speech at Gettysburg lasted only two minutes.

Ulysses S. Grant

(1822–1885)

Ulysses S. Grant, born in Ohio, attended the U.S. Military Academy at West Point, New York. He served in the army and then returned to live in Missouri. When President Lincoln called for volunteer soldiers in 1861, Grant stepped forward. He was a brilliant leader. In 1864 Lincoln appointed him commander of the Union Army. The Union's victory made him a national hero. He later served as president of the United States from 1869 to 1877.

Lincoln trusted General Grant.

Lincoln delivered the Gettysburg Address at a Civil War battlefield in November 1863. The speech is only 272 words long, but it is considered the most famous speech in U.S. history.

Fact VS. Fiction

In a 1906 book called *The Perfect Tribute*, Mary Shipman Andrews wrote that Lincoln composed the Gettysburg Address on the back of an envelope while traveling to Gettysburg on a train. Andrew's book sold 500,000 copies. People still believe the story, but it isn't true. Lincoln wrote the speech before he left Washington, D.C. He probably practiced it on the train.

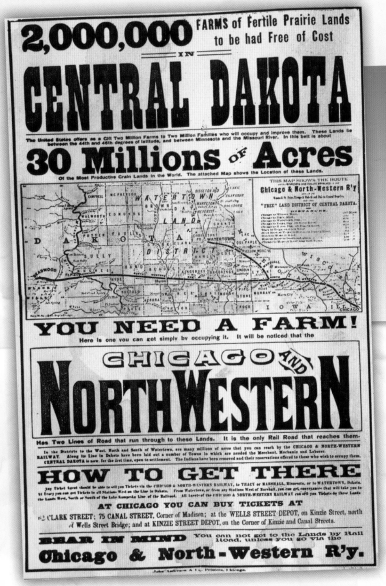

This poster, published by the Chicago and North-western Railroad, advertised free land for homesteaders in Dakota Territory.

The Homestead Act

The Civil War took up most of Lincoln's time, but like all presidents, he also dealt with other nations and other issues affecting the United States. In 1862 he signed the Homestead Act. This act allowed citizens to claim 160-acre (65-hectare) plots of land in the West. It required **homesteaders** to live on the land, build a house, and farm the land for five years before taking ownership. The Homestead Act was a creative way to develop new settlements. Eventually homesteaders settled about 10 percent of all the land in the United States.

Reelection

Lincoln's supporters began to ask about a second term as president. Was Lincoln interested? Yes. He wanted to end the war and reunite the country. However, after years of war and a terrible loss of life, many people opposed Lincoln. The **Democrats** selected General McClellan as their candidate. Lincoln prepared for defeat.

But good news from the battlefields helped Lincoln win the election. The Union Navy took control of Mobile Bay in Alabama. Atlanta, Georgia, fell to General Sherman. And General Sheridan won battles in Virginia. Voters approved of Lincoln's actions. Among Union soldiers, more than 70 percent voted for Lincoln. Lincoln felt confident about the future.

This photo shows President Lincoln (left) meeting with General George McClellan (right) in his tent near Antietam, Maryland.

The Happiest Days...
and the Saddest

When he was **inaugurated** in March 1865, Lincoln spoke of going forward as a nation "with **malice** toward none, with charity for all." He wanted to reunite the nation peacefully. Many in the audience wept.

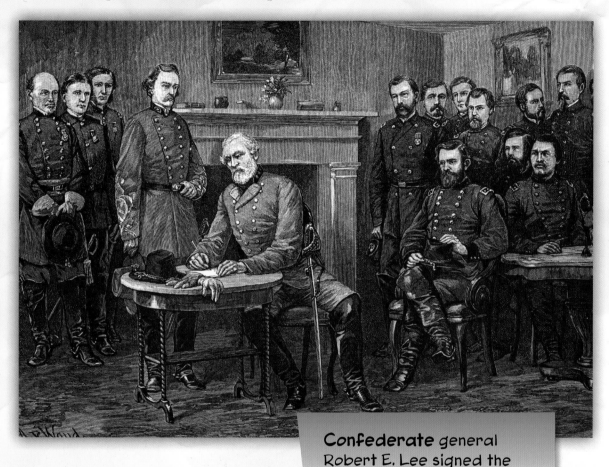

Confederate general Robert E. Lee signed the surrender on April 9, 1865.

On April 3 **Union** troops seized Richmond, Virginia. Lincoln and his son Tad went there. People recognized the president. One woman cried out: "I know that I am free, for I have seen Father Abraham." The city's black citizens surrounded Lincoln and touched his clothing. A few days later the war ended.

The last day

On April 14 President Lincoln looked forward to "four years of peace and happiness" during his second term. That evening he and Mary attended a play at Ford's Theater. When they entered the theater, the crowd cheered. Lincoln bowed to the audience and took his place.

During the third act of the play, an actor named John Wilkes Booth (see box on page 39) quietly entered Lincoln's theater box. He aimed his pistol at the back of the Lincoln's head and pulled the trigger. Lincoln slumped forward, gravely injured.

Booth walked past the guard's empty chair, directly to Lincoln's theater box.

His final hours

Mary screamed. Army major Henry Rathbone, who was seated next to Lincoln, rose to attack Booth. But Booth was faster. He slashed the major with a dagger and then jumped down onto the stage.

The audience was stunned. People raced to the exits. Men carried the wounded president to a boarding house across the street. A doctor examined him, shook his head, and said that Lincoln would not survive. Lincoln's friends and advisers stayed throughout the night, but Lincoln never opened his eyes.

Paintings often show family and advisers gathered around Lincoln's deathbed. But the room was not big enough to hold this many people. Tad was never there.

John Wilkes Booth was a popular actor.

John Wilkes Booth

(1838–1865)

John Wilkes Booth, who was born in Maryland, believed in the Confederate cause. He organized a team to help him kidnap Lincoln, whom he hated. That plan fell apart, so in 1865 he decided to kill Lincoln himself. This time he succeeded. Booth broke his leg when he jumped from the theater box. He died a few days later when Union troops surrounded his hiding place and one of them shot him.

Abraham Lincoln died around 7:00 a.m. the next morning. Those in the room knelt by the bed while a minister prayed. After a moment of silence, Secretary of War Edward Stanton declared, "Now he belongs to the ages."

Manhunt

The hunt for Booth and those who helped him began immediately. It took Union soldiers 12 days to find Booth. They finally found him hiding at a Virginia farm. Booth's last words were: "I did what I thought was best."

Did you know?

Lincoln's birthday is a state holiday in Connecticut, Illinois, Missouri, New Jersey, and New York. Indiana and New Mexico celebrate Lincoln Day in November. In 1971 President Richard Nixon combined the birthdays of George Washington and Abraham Lincoln into a national holiday called Presidents' Day. It is celebrated on the third Monday in February.

A Nation Remembers

After Lincoln's **assassination**, people praised his great accomplishments. During 1865–1866, over 450 pamphlets and speeches were printed in praise of Lincoln. People began writing biographies and creating legends about Lincoln— some fact, others fiction.

Unfortunately, Lincoln's violent death killed his idea of peace "with **malice** toward none, with charity for all." The period that followed the Civil War, called **Reconstruction**, brought about many difficult changes in the South. Hard feelings between the North and South continued for decades.

Thousands of people attended funeral parades for Lincoln, such as this one in Washington, D.C. Parades were held in nine other major cities.

The statue of Lincoln inside the Lincoln Memorial is 19 feet (5.8 meters) high and weighs 175 tons (159 tonnes).

Lincoln's place in history

Today, Lincoln is remembered for saving the nation and freeing the slaves. The Lincoln Memorial in Washington, D.C., was opened in 1922. Millions of people visit it each year. There are five other sites run by the National Park Service that honor Lincoln (see "Places to visit" on page 47). At Mount Rushmore in South Dakota, Lincoln's face is carved into the mountain beside the faces of three other presidents. Whether he is called "Honest Abe," "Father Abraham," or the "Great **Emancipator**," Abraham Lincoln holds a special place in U.S. history.

Fact VS. Fiction

Some people believe that **Confederate** General Robert E. Lee's profile is carved onto the back of Lincoln's marble head—or perhaps hidden in his stone hair—at the Lincoln Memorial. This is not true, but the story lives on.

Timeline

1809
Abraham Lincoln is born on February 12 in Hardin County (now LaRue County), Kentucky.

1811
The Lincoln family moves to Hodgenville, Kentucky.

1818
Lincoln's mother, Nancy, dies at age 34 in Spencer County, Indiana.

1819
Lincoln's father marries Sarah Bush Johnston.

1828
Lincoln takes a flatboat to New Orleans.

1836
Lincoln receives his law license.

1834
Lincoln is elected to the Illinois state legislature.

1833
Lincoln opens a store in New Salem. Lincoln also becomes postmaster.

1832
Lincoln serves as a captain in the Black Hawk War.

1830
The Lincoln family moves to Illinois. A year later, Abraham settles in New Salem, Illinois.

1837
Lincoln moves to Springfield, Illinois. He meets Joshua Speed there.

1842
Lincoln marries Mary Todd in Springfield.

1843
Robert Todd Lincoln is born in Springfield.

1846
Edward Baker Lincoln is born in Springfield. Lincoln is elected to the U.S. Congress.

1858
Abraham Lincoln and Stephen A. Douglas debate one another while running for the U.S. Senate.

1855
Lincoln runs for the U.S. Senate but loses.

1853
Thomas (Tad) Lincoln is born in Springfield.

1850
Edward dies at age three. William Wallace Lincoln is born in Springfield.

1860
Republicans choose Lincoln as their presidential candidate. Lincoln is elected president of the United States.

1861
Lincoln is inaugurated. Meanwhile, some states begin to leave the Union to form the Confederate States of America.

1862
Willie Lincoln dies. Lincoln writes the Emancipation Proclamation.

1865
In January Congress approves the 13th Amendment, which ends slavery. On April 9, Confederate General Robert E. Lee surrenders.

On April 14, John Wilkes Booth shoots Lincoln. On April 15, Lincoln dies from his wounds.

1864
Lincoln is reelected president.

1863
Lincoln issues the Emancipation Proclamation. He also delivers the Gettysburg Address.

Family Tree

Thomas Lincoln (1778-1851) = Nancy Hanks Lincoln (1784-1818)

Robert Smith Todd (1791-1849) = Eliza Ann Parker (1794-1825)

Abraham Lincoln (1809-1865) = Mary Todd Lincoln (1818-1882)

Robert Lincoln (1843-1926)

Edward Lincoln (1846-1850)

William Lincoln (1850-1862)

Thomas Lincoln (1853-1871)

Mary "Mamie" Lincoln (1869-1938)

Abraham Lincoln II (1873-1890)

Jessie Harlan Lincoln (1875-1948)

Glossary

assassination murder of a political figure in a surprise attack

campaign competition between candidates for political office

circuit court state court holding sessions in different areas of a district or region

Confederacy group of 11 southern states that seceded from the United States in 1860–1861; *see also* Confederate States of America

Confederate person who supported the Confederate States of America

Confederate States of America states that seceded from the United States in 1860–1861; *see also* Confederacy

debt something that is owed

Democrat member of the political party that arose in the 1820s from a split in the Democratic-Republican Party

emancipation act of freeing someone, such as a slave

emancipator someone who frees a slave

endure to last or survive

flatboat large, flat-bottomed boat used on rivers

homesteader settler who lays claim to land given by the government

inaugurate to officially place someone in office

legislature group of people who have the responsibility and power to make the laws for a country or state

malice evil or the desire to cause harm

militia army made up of volunteer soldiers

patent license for an invention

postmaster official in charge of a post office

Reconstruction process by which the states that had seceded were reorganized as part of the Union after the Civil War

replica close or exact copy of something

Republican member of a political party that began in 1854 to oppose slavery

secede make a formal withdrawal of membership; during the Civil War, the Confederate states seceded from the United States

shabby worn; showing signs of neglect

slavery relationship in which one person has absolute power over another and controls his or her life, liberty, and fortune

surveyor official who measures, values, or maps land areas

Union another word for the United States of America; during the Civil War, the term was used to mean those states that did not secede

Whig member of a political party (about 1834 to 1855) that was formed to oppose the Democratic Party

widow woman whose husband has died

Find Out More

Books

Allen, Thomas B., and Roger MacBride Allen. *Mr. Lincoln's High-Tech War: How the North Used the Telegraph, Railroads, Surveillance Balloons, Ironclads, High-powered Weapons, and More to Win the Civil War*. Washington, D.C.: National Geographic, 2009.

Hankins, Chelsey. *The Lincoln Memorial*. New York: Chelsea Clubhouse, 2010.

Krull, Kathleen. *Lincoln Tells a Joke: How Laughter Saved the President (and the Country)*. Boston: Houghton Mifflin Harcourt, 2010.

Waldman, Neil. *Voyages: Reminiscences of Young Abe Lincoln*. Honesdale, Pa.: Calkins Creek, 2009.

DVDs

Abraham Lincoln Comes Home. Spoken Arts, 2009.

Lincoln: His Life and Legacy. A&E Television, 2008.

Websites

Abraham Lincoln Presidential Library and Museum
www.alplm.org/timeline/timeline.html
Follow a timeline of major events in Lincoln's life.

Abraham Lincoln Research Site
http://rogerjnorton.com/Lincoln2.html
This site, by an American history teacher, offers a variety of resources about Abraham Lincoln for students and teachers.

Getting to Know Abraham Lincoln
http://kids.librarypoint.org/abraham_lincoln
Learn about Lincoln at this library website.

The White House Presidents Site
www.whitehouse.gov/about/presidents/
This site provides brief biographies of every United States president.

The Gettysburg Address at the Smithsonian
http://americanhistory.si.edu/documentsgallery/exhibitions/
gettysburg_address_1.html
Learn more about the Gettysburg Address and download a copy.

Places to visit

Abraham Lincoln Birthplace National Historic Site
2995 Lincoln Farm Road
Hodgenville, KY 42748
www.nps.gov/abli/index.htm

Abraham Lincoln Memorial
Lincoln Memorial Circle
Washington, DC 20024
www.nps.gov/linc/index.htm

Ford's Theatre
511 10th Street NW
Washington, DC 20004
www.nps.gov/foth/index.htm

Gettysburg Battlefield
1195 Baltimore Pike
Gettysburg, PA 17325
www.nps.gov/gett/index.htm

Lincoln Boyhood National Memorial
2916 East South Street
Lincoln City, IN 47552
www.nps.gov/libo/index.htm

Lincoln Home National Historic Site
413 South 8th Street
Springfield, IL 62701
www.nps.gov/liho/index.htm

Index